Ragged Robin's Rhymes

By Robert Goodwin Olmsted
Edited by Charlaine Taylor

Ragged Robin's Rhymes

Metaphors 4 Life
The HeArt of Language
Building and empowering lives and communities through the oral, written, visual and kinesthetic languages.
www.danarondel.com

This book is a work of poetry.

Published by Metaphors 4 Life 2009
Cover Design by Dana Rondel

ISBN: 978-0-9817291-2-1
ISBN: 0-9817291-2-6

This book is printed on acid-free paper. Printed in the United States of America.

This book is dedicated to
family and friends.

Table of Contents
Ragged Robin's Rhymes

Poetry by Robert Goodwin Olmsted
Contributing Writer and Editor, Charlaine Taylor
Contributing Writer, Dorothy A. Wilkerson

Fox's Clock

An astute Mr. Fox
Owned umpteen clocks,
All of which showed the proper time.

All but for one
Which he said was no fun,
Because all that it did was chime.

And no one knew when
It might sound in the den
Or just when or what way to rewind.

So, that clock he abhorred.
Besides it had no cord,
Because it wasn't the 'lectric kind.

He said it was wrong,
The way it would gong
Without any reason or rhyme,

The hands moved at a fitful pace
On a broken face,
He sold the clock for a nifty dime.

Then he said, “That's done!”
But in time he grew glum
For not hearing that odd fickle chime.

He became so bored
Without the clock he'd abhorred,
That he practically lost his mind.

And because of its lack,
As Mr. Fox looked back,
For that clock night and day he would pine.

What he then wanted most
Was to give up the ghost;
But they kept him kicking with quinine and lime.

And he finally said
On his assumed death bed,
"Selling that clock was a cowardly crime."

Then oddly, that old clock turned up with a bum,
Who offered it back for a sum,
Two fairly good bottles of muscatel wine.

Despite the dear cost,
The clock he'd feared lost
Somehow now showed the proper time,

Which just then
Was four minutes to ten,
Or perhaps it was fifty-six past nine.

It had needed repair,
Having sustained much wear,
But the clock's workings were at last in line,

And the chimes sounded when
They were supposed to have been;
Their chords were pure and exquisitely fine.

Fox jumped from his bed.
"My good friend," he said,
"Before you leave, you must dine!"

The bum had a meal.
And the muscatel sealed the deal.
With the bum's terse words: "That clock keeps good time."

As I needn't explain,
Fox had felt much pain;
Till he grabbed the clock and proclaiming," This clock's mine!"

Since then all the while
He's been wearing a smile,
The clock's timely, "chime" finally ends this rhyme.

Of Autumn's Birds and Leaves

Like flighty birds flocked in trees awaiting,
A parting time to begin migrating,
Fall leafs shake on the boughs of their trees,
Until comes along a more cogent breeze.
And away fly fall leaves, oft quite a few,
Like birds which a few weeks ago flew too.

Under the lone sun, our sole parent star,
Copious currents circulate and are
Blowing leafs around far away and nigh.
Round the woods and fields, buoyant in the sky,
Seeming to be blithely having a heyday,
While to desist, they've neither call nor way.

As temperatures dwindle, early in fall,
And feeling chill air, the birds not to loll
Fix to fly south. As if that weren't enough,
Forsaking autumn leaves is but more tough.
Expectation makes the waiting birds cheep,
Who flit and twitter the while willows weep.

Through dangling stems the whining wind you'll hear,
Wind which also chases leaves far and near.
Leaves from maples, oaks, willows, pick your trees,
Elms, cherries, tulips, ashes, hickories,
Glide down breezes, to gild earth with their hues,
All the rainbow's colors, except for blues.

Senseless fall leaves don't know when they are old,
And are oblivious when it gets cold.
Judge these beliefs and disclose right away,
Whether they're correct, if maybe yes, hey!
One and twelve boney crows baked in a pie
Might proffer reasons to try a piece high.

After the pie is opened up just right,
Baked crows are heard all cawing day and night.
Serve the pie; though the crows weren't inspected,
Just bear in mind, that fowl luck accepted
Might mean a meal not missed, and mark these words:
Not often flatly flavored are free birds.

Barefoot In Favor of Tile

Some wooden boards
Make good floors,
Although one can deliver
A very painful sliver.
Cement may be strong
And lasts pretty long
But without a buffer
Can cause one to suffer.
Some advocate rugs,
And others say carpet.
I've heard they harbor bugs
But doubt they'll leave the market.
At last, it's linoleum tile
Which compels me so to smile.
Though it's often redundantly square,
My feet require less special care.

Homestretch

On a desolate central city street
Through the dreary, drizzling April night
Came one of three living souls in sight:
A lonely, self-occupied ole policeman,
And when he stopped me, I asked him,
"Have you ten cents and the time?"
He replied, "A quarter to eleven."
And, "Yes, I've got a dime,"
Then he asked, "What's the money for?"
I told him, "Coffee in the morn."
"Oh well, that's OK and fine.
Have a couple quarters more!
Then he asked me, "Where you from?"
And I told him, "West coast shore."
"Well, get yourself back home."
He said and left me there alone,
I tightened up a soggy shoe;
I had to pound the pavement too.
Not then a ride I'd try to bum;
When out of town, I'd start to thumb.
So far a car had yet to show.
Before the morning few drove past,
And I had five hundred miles to go,
Before I'd get on home at last.

A Ding-A-Ling Heading Into Winter

Ding-a-Ling
Heading
Into Winter
In the month of November
This afternoon at a quarter past two,
I checked for my mail which I usually do.
As I cracked my front door, in blew real chilly air
Announcing: Indian summer's 'bout done out there.
Opening it further fetched red leaves with the wind,
Harbingers of wimp winter thought I, and I grinned.
Looking to the woods whence the leaves had come,
I could see some lovelies that had actually sinned,
Could make out which trees those leaves were from,
For their supple, taupe limbs were lewdly exposed.
How ludicrous, thought I, how laughable and dumb.
I'm more modest and wiser than trees, I proposed,
Yet as ice and snow begin to fall along with degrees,
I had best not be too far-out nor smug nor reposed;
No, but wary as that wimp winter may not aim to please.
I must keep doors and windows very tightly closed.
Merely time-tested tenets of real wisdom are these
And from now on outdoors I should be suitably clothed,
Not undressed like the autumn's ridiculous trees,
Which are just being as anyone would have supposed;
The conduct of people and of trees performing striptease
Are divergent matters not ever meant to be transposed,
And I mustn't go streaking down north past October, lest I freeze.
N'est pas?
Oui!

November Leaves

As flocked birds wait in their tree way stations
To proceed with their great migrations,
Gold leafs clinging to their less mortal trees
Vacillate, till blows a decisive breeze.
And not sensing the chill factor at all
Off fly flights of freed leafs like fowl; it's fall.

Foggy Bog Stew

It seems odder by far than turtles in treetops,
That some connoisseurs choose just soup
At mealtime to sup
And sadder than ice cubes in barbecue pits
That for others only porridge or chowder will do.

It may be a bit cloudier but to gather a group,
It's foggy bog stew that I like to brew.

I shouldn't divulge the recipe,
But let me let you in on a secret please:
It's made with stray strips of stale mutton,
Moldy, gray marshmallows, hundred proof gin
Blue pickled toads and dead spider chins.
Add a kilo, corn whiskey, three different teas
And a dozen turned taters per pot,
Horseflies, brown beetles and dismembered bees,
No barley but lice and don't stop.
Add a dash in each pot of ol' devil's tail spice
Which will help...should suffice.

It's really quite solemnly dismal and nice, the rot
As it's stirred with an old sock fit trim
On a stick and re-stirred pot by pot
All swashin' and bubblin' o'er each trembling brim
And into the fire drop by drop
With clouds of thick steam
Rising on up, mushrooming out all about,
Out up into the fog
From under the edges
Of each rattly top.

Inside a circle of occupied logs,
Occupied, yes indeed, all by gourmet elite
On an odd half acre of mud, brambles and peat,
There beneath a great bumblebush tree
Spreading high also over the plot
This cuisine is conceived,
It's fragrance perceived
On each passing breeze
Near the far away lot.

I do like foggy bog stew
And so very much too:
Delicious to taste
And easy to chew
Served only to us,
A select crew.

If you would, tell me, please do,
Could it possibly not
Be not at all true
You would possibly not
Like it very well too,
Were it served piping hot
Just to me and a few
At that special spot
Including you?

The Wind And A Gnome

For naught
But one gnome
Seeks the wind.
For one gnome alone
The wind is seeking,
And she shrieks.
Shrieking She speaks
Hoping to reach
One lost gnome.
Frantically peaking
She ceases then seeks.
Now in holes, then in hollows,
In meadows and treetops,
In trees She is ringing
And in haylofts.
In grasses She's singing
To be heard by one gnome,
And not hearing his song
She complains and She whines.
Unwinding
She whistles and whispers
In search of one gnome.
For one gnome
She stalls.
For one gnome
She calls,
Then She waits
For one gnome,
And beginning again
She wails,
And She screams
Increasing, still seeking
To cease again
And to cry again.
She dies again.
Lonesome, she listens
To hear one lone gnome,
And hearing no sound,
She goes home-
Once again goes on home
Not having found
One lost gnome.

To Bear a Cross

Round and round the oak tree they twine,
The rapacious appendages of a poison ivy vine.
The aged tree stands tall and firm but unseen
In a smothering of spades virulent dark green.
The undaunted host to the insidious weed
Is apparently somehow prevailing indeed,
Though it's obscure where the poison vine starts
And where in its windings some places it parts.
The tree shows sparse patches of healthy oak leaves
Not fully eclipsed by the parasite as it weaves,
And in the oak's strength it reaches high and proud
Supporting the sheer weight of the vine but unbowed.
If in a lifetime we were beset like that tree,
In remote ways like that shackled, not free,
We might hope to endure too, majestic and strong
And bear up with that cross no matter how long.

my jade plant an abridged poem

it took up a pot
on my window sill
and adores the spot
is living there still

found as a sprout
down in the trash
now reaches out
to skirt the sash

and kiss the wall
not jack s beanstalk
but two feet tall
and there s been talk

won't reach the sky
the way it bows
but it oh my
a twisting goes

Night Moth

As I paced about my room bemused and in a quandary,
I opened up a window and observed the moonlit foundry,
Then just about an hour ago this very night, you see,
A lone and unknown night moth came to call on me.
Back and forth he flew before my disbelieving face
Flitting rather madly much as if to win a race,
With, it seemed, some pressing message to convey.
Of course, I wondered what it was he had to say,
Until some moments later as he dipped and hovered,
'Twas not a message but two queries, I discovered:
"How be ye here? What is this your life to thee?"
Was what I sensed him very plainly asking me.
After thought I answered not too loud but clear,
"My meek and minimal friend, please do not fear;
For me to be here at this time is suitable and right,
Though I live most by day, and you live most at night."
And,"I am very pleased with this, my humble life, you know.
I do wonder when the likes of you comes by to visit, though.
Living out our discrete lives should take us each our distances"
And then also, "I'm glad to make you one of my acquaintances,
However, it behooves me now to show you nicely to the door.
You see, I don't recall that we have ever met this way before."
My curt but pondered answers seemed to have him satisfied;
Before he fluttered off a bit then out, he looked most gratified.

betty grable

on a maple
bedside table
in our room
my cactus plant
would like to bloom
yet she can't
don't ask why
perhaps she's shy
but maybe later
if I sate her
with some water
she'll be able
to deck the table
with a blossom
which would
be awesome
still she seems to
have no need to
have much nurture
too much water
enervates her
but the sun shines
in and oft-times
stimulates her
motivates her
if I leave her
forever after
i will grieve her
she's so pretty
i'll call her betty
betty grable
she'll soon be able

The Tree

I saw an old tree deep, deep in a wood
Which was clearly not there for any good.
Its bole was quite huge and undulant,
Its bark like the hide of an elephant.
It looked at a glance much like other trees,
Till it twisted and swayed without any breeze.
As if claws of wild falcons were grafted there,
Its branches would grope and clutch at the air.
A prime bough could flex like a living snake,
While a beast it would grip and readily take,
Then strangulate live until thoroughly dead,
To stuff in a mouth which had not a head,
A mouth, quite obscured by divergent limbs
Up on the trunk . . . here, my memory dims,
But I recall how it moved sensing some prey
Close at hand to dispatch and ingest that way.
But for a rabbit which hopped in too near,
I wouldn't have known enough to have fear,
I watched as it took more poor creatures alive,
A fox, a lone deer . . . how it did thrive!
I observed from a distance for quite some time,
And am urged to inform you using this rhyme,
Lest you wander unwittingly off and away
And deep into that wood some very sad day.

Sweet Song

Solitary blackbird
Sitting in a tree,
Your sweet song I heard;
.Was it just for me?

While Off In Your Fastness

Oh, where enchantress,
Where have you gone?
Off to your fastness
Where naught can be wrong.

All in a fortnight
Your love slipped away.
Now is the daylight
A dead shade of gray.

When we were one,
You were all life to me.
Now that you're gone,
I've no reason to be

If you'd return,
My heart would rejoice;
Not vainly I'd yearn
For the sound of your voicc.

If you were here again,
Anew I would heed
Your dancing eyes keen,
Your tender beauty.

Why don't you need me
In the way that I dream?
Why won't you meet me
Our worlds in between?

You'd be my fair mistress;
We'd share a love
Blessed with the fullness
Of heaven above.

I'll bide my lonesomeness
These long nights and days,
As in my consciousness
Your sweet memory stays.

Oh, where enchantress,
Where have you gone?
Off to your fastness
Where naught can be wrong.

Preface To The Witch, The Kids And The Dooomketch

To preface the story
While excluding facts gory
The writer offers here this brief word of record:

The Dooomketch was found
Off of Long Island Sound
Without a sole surviving human on board.

A pirate's boat
Astray but afloat,
She carried naught but bare bones and a sword.

By this name she's been renowned
Since on the hull seamen found
The letters: DOOOMKETCH obscured port and starboard,

But from then till present day
There has been no sure way
To establish a true owner or shiplord.

So she's left to who's able
To sail a ship that's a fable,
Or to whomever she is by chance offered,

But few there have been
Who would sail her again,
Since she was found off The Sound drifting seaward.

She will sometimes seem
To have been a mere dream
And is said to show up and disappear as if conjured.

She's spied most near the coast,
A ghost ship people boast,
Spectral, eerie and often just anchored.

The Witch, The Kids And The Dooomketch

In a house with a thatch
Enclosed by a pumpkin patch
Within a forest which was later New London's

Primeval, as it were,
With cougar and bear
Sometime in the mid-sixteen hundreds

There lived a vile witch
Entrusted to watch
Poor settlers' all too misunderstood young ones.

Lank but strong was that witch.
Her broom shaft was a stiff switch,
Which she frequently used on those wronged ones.

They weren't yet old
Enough to scold,
So she'd brooomswitch rather than chide them.

When they got in her path,
She'd show them her wrath,
Brooomswitch outright, strip, tan and then hide them.

And she captured their pets
With traps, snares and nets,
Cut them in pieces and fried them.

With innocence and couth
They would tell her the truth,
But she just questioned, tested and tried them

Then out tripping was she
Five nights and days, five or three.
She brought back poison salves and applied them.

Very fast she would fly on her brooomswitch too high
And make them all cry,
Because she just couldn't abide them.

They wouldn't complain,
Place guilt or blame,
But she'd still taunt, shame and ride them.

Though they prayed she'd desist,
She'd only persist
And to add to her evil with leather she tied them.

Before ending a day
By having her way,
She'd tie them together and leave them.

'Neath a moon of green cheeese
She'd ride her brooomswitch o'er the seas
After down on their knees she had fleeced them.

This she did through the years
Enjoying their tears
Not seeing their growth as she teased them.

Then she absconded one morning.
Against her hard warning
They united themselves which released them.

They worked the hide loose
And tied a hangman's noose
With which to lasso the brooomswitch and ground her.

They set sail on a boat,
The Dooomketch, you'll note
With a notion to hunt down and find her.

The craft came from hell
And would itself propel
Without wind lest the witch ply her magic.

After a mile,
Having traveled awhile,
The Dooomketch seemed awfully lethargic,

But they remained underway,
Though, needless to say,
The witch had cut the wind with her static.

She saw them first slowly approaching,
On her near vicinity encroaching
The outcome she feared would be tragic.

They reasoned, of course,
To keep the witch, that gaunt horse,
In one piece would be a worthy object.

And they also all thought,
She'd surely be caught,
If they roped the haft of the shaft for a ringer.

The other resorts
Were the unpleasant sorts.
By the throat or the feet would just end her.

They chose not to harm,
Just to catch and disarm
And were afraid they might slip up and drown her.

Then they spied her offshore,
A hundred yards or more.
Their brazen attack would astound her.

The closer they got,
Within earshot
The more they feared they'd upend her,

And they decided and tried
To disregard her pride
By giving her a chance to surrender,

A boy climbed the mast
And hollered,"Avast!"
Which seemed to do naught but offend her,

And she concocted bad weather,
Still, they cast up the leather
And would have caught the handle and downed her,

But the first two lobs of the noose
Grazed the witch falling loose;
The third struck pure gold and they owned her.

Every overjoyed kid
Pulled on the tether, he did
To bring the witch in to capture and bind her.

They pulled and tugged away,
A Dooomketch heyday,
Till oddly the ship began to pitch and to founder.

The boat shivered and shook
As if shocked and mistook.
And, as if on a hell-bent bender.

In the violent commotion
The witch fell in the ocean
Missing the deck of the Dooomketch to flounder.

When she sank in the brew,
It seemed to end the to-do,
But the fit had nearly split the old ship asunder.

Being sadly too thin,
She was unable to swim,
As demise in the cold drink found her,

And what followed at last,
As the incident passed
Was a lightning flash and a clap of loud thunder.

Though they were very dismayed,
For her crimes she had paid,
So this story is a sort of happy ender.

But if or not you're a witch,
Beware who you switch;
Retribution could be even sounder.

Mother Earth Around Summer Solstice

She flits and flirts with everyone around,
Lush and verdant flora her luxuriant gown
Outside a pure translucent saline water slip
Which about her curvy self quite nicely fits.
When after spring's rebirth has come and gone,
If her garb's not ripped, she's full of life and gay.
In her vast and viscous liquid depths way down,
And on the same unbounded main with waves,
At its ebbed edges' sands and there beyond,
And in her inland and backwater lakes she stays.
In shallow pools, in reservoirs and passive ponds,
Joining tributary passages and winding waterways,
In skies and landlocked seas, on sloping banks
With scattered rocks at ends of land also she plays,
About her facing cliffs in shelved terrace pans,
All throughout her open, spreading plains beneath
Which reach to cling at lofty mountains peaked
And penetrating thunderheads conceiving rain,
That drenches fields and woods . . . to drain
Filling up to flooding slow moving and meandering
Or profoundly fast and furious river ways in time
To facilitate felicitating, flitting fishes most benign.
From each humble hole and hollow, nest and hive,
Their fissures, cracks and crevices and caves, alive
Other beings, insects, birds, amphibia and beasts
Come to party, as to them she bends her supple knees.
On dunes and windy hilltops high all night and day
And on wafted prairies wide and lightly waved,
In valleys' bottoms fruitfully embellished after May,
Plants and animals with her at one, prevail.

Unmeasured and collective waters
From fresh celestial rain that drives,
Fill up open vessel bodies where
Her beings draw in part their lots and lives.
The residuum to evaporate or flow
From springs in rivulets and brooks to fill
Up creeks to tumble, run and spill
To bubble, froth and rise and fall
Away articulating turns to curl
In current eddies twist and swirl;
Then hasten with a gay melodic purl
Through subterranean passages

And out again. It trips on still
In divined and certain courses never ending,
Between her rivers' banking arms extending,
Through their old deltoid mouths expanding,
To rush past crusted offshore shelves expending,
Till at last its open ocean seas
In sloshy and impossibly unbreaking waves it breaches.
There well beyond her salted sandy beaches
And unvirulent and teaming coastal wetland reaches
Her mammal fish and birds of sea
May call or cry and sing in shrieks and screeches.
In her inshore woodlands too she lives;
There she also learns and teaches.
On roofed and spacey chambered
Green mansions' floors she's seated,
In lowly forest rooms self-constructing
With pertinent and wisely if rudely interrupting,
Bumpy logs and ruts and holes and quicksand ditches,
Mounds with molds and whippy sticks for witches,
Shafts with thorns and snappy switches upwardly extruded,
There too she may be greeted.
Imperviously shy, she's not to be too much upon obtruded,
Nor her sanctuary palaces too much into intruded.
In places where she stands
'Mid stately proud and humble caryatid boles.
Their supported untruncated boughs
Undulantly upstretching throw
Outreaching, clutching limbs and branches groping
And arranging indescribably in complex and meshing
odd phalanxes.
Draped often shrouded with light and dainty lacy veils
Of twined twigs and tiny dangling lances.
Elfin and viridian phalanges
Seemingly instruct, while protecting
The well surveyed, from high above
Low slowly curling, green, fern fronds
In grasses 'round mossy stones with mini-plants
And creeping vines and maybe little mice,
Hidden snakes and frogs and slugs and tiny lice.
Beseechingly, not in despair, and untenaciously,
With slight ungrasping fingers her small and her mighty
Well known trees extend their varietal cones and nuts
and comic corns.
Not to philander offer they their bitter buds and sharp,
tart leaves,
Their early decorous flowery wreaths

Before minute ungerminated spores and pollen seeds
To ride the wind or teasing bees
Can hook a ride for free to leave
And find the homes they need
To incubate and grow and breed.

And maybe later every fruited tree
Its bounteous produce generously releases
With citrus, apples, sundry nuts and even peaches.
If some from cultivated crops, beets, carrots, beans and peas
And some nuts and fruits are spared, not hoarded or invested,
Then, with these her other friends may well be treated,
Of many extra ones her plants are quick to be divested.
And in the covert bosom shield
Of each bush and shrub and tree,
In every water body, wood and field
As in many another sphere
She feeds her fauna all with equal care and glee.

And when in time they're partied out,
And out she is of all her best,
About a maybe matter lending doubt,
She may end at length a spatting bout.
When they are worn and tired but fed,
She gives her creatures needed and deep seated rest,
To shelter draws them closely to her chest,
And then alone, alone awake and gripped
With sullen agonizing clouded fits,
Because the moon and stars at night
And the glowing giver of daylight
Don't seem to shine for them beneath.
She sheds in sorrow-laden sheets
Her hapless tears of mournful grief,
Not slow or light or few or brief;
She weeps profusely on her dress
Until completely soaking wet
To wash and wash the shame of it,
Until she ceases late to fret.
For skies have turned quite brightly new,
All sunny and a lovely shade of blue.
Her sopping frock she dries all through,
Then sports it once again for you
With maybe, yes, a rainbow band or two.

But watch her carefully from the start;
With her sharp hay fever, "'shoo!"
Since it's gettin' pretty hot in every part,
She'll have you sneeze a little and a lot,.
And make you blush and too much too.

As days grow shorter and until her summertime is out;
She then as ever tends and tames and nurses life about.
In every half she reigns all times and ways supreme,
But before she changes her role from summer queen
She may not bend to loose a cooling gust or breeze,
For spells of dull dog days, nor shed a single drop of rain to glean,
But she might, if mounted heat remains too long at high degree
Enlist El Viento, Le Vent, The Wind, and/or Foggy Mist to it relieve.
And if appeased, she'll bless each one with sweet ineffability
As when throughout her wild and mild and flowering realms,
Her mountain meadows, marshy swamps and forest glens,
As born upon their reaching, branches, stalks and stems
Now courtly and abundant self-expressing blossoms
Attended by their sleekly verte and gladly waving friends,
While wafted with her warm capricious summer winds
Dance, ecstatic, as if on toward their sought for
Grand and grave, great, fructuous ends.

Two Odes To A Housefly

1

Why so hurried, little guest,
As you race across my chest?
I am of the tender type,
Yet you scurry so inclined
To put me to this vexing test,
And I am loath to make a swipe
Preferring not to be unkind,
So you can flit elsewhere, you pest,
For I'm becoming really ripe
To bide and strike, I'll bet you'll find.

2

Narrow escape artist, rascal fly,
Who too wants not today to die,
Who flew on off to buzz around,
And light again upon my thigh,
Whereto you sense that you are bound,
I can only try surmise,
But if you have wee cares and strife,
To match your wee life span and size,
Your brief and tiny, hurried life
With man's one might analogize.

Tune Of June

Bugs and bees
Invade the trees.
To beat the heat
I need a breeze.
Pesky hay fever
Has me sneeze.

For My Valentine 2

I do love
Just you all the time
And hope it's no crime
In this poor little rhyme
To tell you, you're fine
And ask, valentine,
Will you please
Be mine
?

Explication

While having right here and now to do so
Causes my face to blush brilliant red so,
For your kind forbearance I have to ask,
As I start upon this besetting task.

You see, I've racked and racked my feeble brain
For the inkling of a good rhyme to pen,
But I ain't thought of a fitting refrain,
Since I don't remember just now quite when.

Though I scratch and scratch my getting bald head
And twiddle all the day my scribbler's thumbs
Without retiring at all to my bed,
No real inspirational lyric comes,

So I cogitate all the night till morn,
While the really inadequate results
Of trying to invoke a nice brainstorm
Are changes in my breath, pallor and pulse.

Then too, I have the doldrums to fight;
It's the pesky devil I have to thank,
The same one who, when I get set to write,
Has me draw a long, unbearable blank.

So I beseech you, please do understand,
While a better poem I would now hand,
I will have to try at some other time
To spin for you a respectable rhyme.

Workaday Blues

Workaday...
Work all day,
Bring home the bread;
Your family of eight
Has got to be fed.
Time to head home;
It's the end of your shift,
But you'd better not roam,
If you get the drift.
It's a short-lived trip,
Half an hour to the door.
Your wife's in the pits:
"Welcome home, you bore."
Bring in the dog,
But step with great care;
Jimmy brought home a frog
And lost it somewhere.
Clean up the house
Before it's too late,
Before your sick spouse
Attacks you with hate.
Pay the kid with the news;
He waits at the door.
You're humming the blues,
'Cause he's asking for more.
Dry baby's tears;
She's cried for an hour.
Her bottle of milk
Evidently is sour.
Get the food on the table,
Then gather the clan.
Bear the din if your able;
Tell yourself that you can.
The day's nearly over;
Put the children to bed.
You're another day older
And more into the red.
Climb into your pj's,
And kiss your poor wife.
Tomorrow's the first day
Of the rest of your life.

Grease and gum

grease and gum
are lots of fun
but not for some
a fly for one
a spider too
please for you
to empathize
it's not just flies
who hate the goo

To A Daddy Long Legs

Daddy long legs,
Your limbs are lithe and strong,
Not like pegs
But super-fine and long
Enough to keep yourself aloft,
As you go where you want to go,
Across my saffron sweater soft
Or then along the garden row.

The First Snowfall

Very nearly every year
Heaven's first snow flakes appear
Falling gently down to earth
Before December twenty-first,
And as they fall they seem to say,
"Old Man Winter is on his way."
Like an awaited bosom friend
Who settles in near autumn's end
To nip each unprotected nose,
And everybody's tootsie toes,
To kiss tender ears and fingers,
Yet the first snow seldom lingers
And may be just enough to tease
Those who employ winter skis;
And to forewarn all and each,
That winter will have its way.
With the old lessons to reteach,
The unprepared will surely pay,
So let us get our snow gear out,
When first snow starts to fall one day,
Because of this there should be little doubt:
At no time soon will we sustain a torrid drought.

A Special One for Wordsworth

As I ponder flowers of Springtimes past and yet to come
There is for me before the rest a very special one.
Raising its happy trumpet ringed with petals bright
Though not too bold it may for glory match the lily white
And make a show that's just as long and just as gay.
Resplendent in late April and through the month of May,
Upon its cheerful beauty all year round I like to dwell,
And, Yes, its name you've guessed: The Golden Daffodil.

Bean Pot Valentine

there is not any crime
in this bean pot rhyme
to write to you valentine
that I think you are fine
and I want you all the time
to please be only mine
without you I just pine

Ice Cream Treat

Come dog days you'll meet
Your good pals, and in luck
You'll each get a treat
To nibble, lick or suck
Something frozen and sweet
From the good humor truck.

Its droll ding-a-ling rings,
And you prick up an ear.
Of chilly goodness, it sings,
As the truck travels near
Packing ice creamy things
To assuage, cool and cheer.

When it makes a quick stop
On your neighborhood street,
Whether bar, cone or pop,
You just know in the heat,
It can drop by wet drop
Embellish both your bare feet.

What you buy looks too small;
And you hope it will last,
But you must eat it all,
As you must eat it fast,
Till happ'ly you can loll,
Once the crisis is past.

If it does melt...good grief.
You need quick a clean plate,
Tissue, cloth, handkerchief,
Now, before it's too late.
Sticky heat's a sneak thief;
What it leaves though is great.

When you root for your team
Doing battle this year
At a town game you'll scream;
Nevertheless, you'll hear,
Vendors hawking ice cream
Really loud, shrill and clear.

So you take out some money:
Three or four, a few bucks
Just to treat your sweet honey
And yourself, because, shucks!
While ice cream can get runny,
You're just wearing your ducks.

Gladly someday you'll greet
Dear old friends and recall,
How you beat the dire heat
In the days before fall
With a cold ice cream treat,
And just had a real ball.

Lines To An Ancient Oak With Winona Whiston

Among your buckled limbs is an ell for every bow,
A trait which could evoke some droll and indulging jokes,
But just who spent more than two centuries to grow
And now stands high above all the other woodland folks?
Who year-round often shelters herbivore, owl and crow,
And who with seasonal changes wears different cloaks,
Spring or summer verdure, earth shades or white modeled snow?
Yes, it's you who, if human, wouldn't steal, lie nor hoax,
Being steadfast ever even as the north winds blow.
Having sprung from an acorn to become a king of oaks,
Mature and majestic tree, you truly steal the show,
Reigning all supreme, for Smokey The Bear never smokes.
And, indeed, you're strong as oak, as everyone does know.

A Midwinter Night's Mystique

The storm will be ending full soon,
As clouds make a vent for the moon.
Buoyant crystal bijoux disperse to and fro,
As they are borne down earthward and about
Dancing snowflake dances in the wistful moon glow.
And as he shines, the man in the moon seems to pout,
While the minute flakes drift into sculpturesque heaps,
The artistic work of the magical snow witch, no doubt,
But we can not have the dreamy white forms for keeps,
And the woeful man in the moon is suppressing a shout,
Because he knows the sun and wind will melt them away.
He ducks behind cloud and coy, out again peeps,
Decides to retire after all, and then in dismay
Pulls a cloud cover over his head and sleeps,
Until he pops out again, and two coyote bay.
Leaving neat prints, a young snow rabbit leaps
Over the drifts which make such a royal display.
Close to an old squirrel amid snowflakes creeps,
Who alone and aloof seems a runaway stray.
The winter wind blows, and an old willow weeps,
While morning nears, and the world turns light gray.
In my soul the scenes sweet quintessence steeps,
Where forever intact and safekept it will stay,
Till summoned from the annals of my memory someday.

You May

There is a poor babe named Peg
Who has a badly crippled leg.
Although she really is poor,
She is thoroughly unsure,
Whether she ought to beg
Or conscientiously pay.
For her leg there is no cure
We're sadder than sad to say.
She often asks if she might beg.
We answered once: "Peg, you pay!"
But always since: "Beg? You may."

Skunky, Skunky

Skunky, Skunky, what're you adoin',
By my back door asnoopin' and afoolin'?
Ain't you been around here long enough
You misbehavin' black-n-white ball of fluff?
Don't you be so nosy, and don't you keep on stinkin'.
'Fore I get my gun, you'd better go, I'm thinkin'.
I've got to close my windows and my door;
Skunky, I don't want to smell you anymore.

A First Snowfall

By Charlaine Taylor, Robert Olmsted and Ed Frederickson

Merrily along we sing the carols of Christmas.
The snow, as we open the door, begins.
The flakes are illuminated by the light of a lamp beside the path.
We look at foot prints in the snow.
Swirling, clinging to our clothes: snowflakes.
Each snowflake has a unique design.
Blue skies are filled with white polka dots,
Which approach us rapidly, as they fall.
These are the short, fleeting days before Christmas,
And this is the first real snowfall,
White covering everything, but a decorated tree
Upon which the flakes all seem to melt.
These are the waiting days, awaiting Christ's birth.
Once a year, each year reenacted over and over,
A small babe lies in a manger, warm
And reaching out to us: " I'm here. I've never left you."
And our arms feel empty and void to hold the gift, a child.
The world is gift wrapped in endless white.

Thicket

Ye old brambly thicket
Which grows close to our house,
Haven to the cricket,
Slug and hare and grouse,

Who live within your boughs
Little can you know,
Their wherefores and hows
And that they need you so.

You feed your berries to the waxwing,
Hide the burrow of the ringed raccoon,
Lend a loft where the peepers can sing
And keep the caterpillar's silk cocoon.

Is it your one true calling
To provide for scads of life,
The winged and the crawling
In abundance and in strife?

If they did not need you
In all the ways they do,
Still the earth would feed you,
Till your term was through,

But like a selfless mama,
Though for yourself you live,
Protecting them from trauma,
Of yourself you give.

Thickets by the dozens
Dot every town and dell,
For our distant cousins,
Each a good hotel.

The Overeater

He whose name I shan't divulge,
Developed a midriff bulge.
It seemed that he always ate
Whatever was on his plate,
After and then before,
He had to have some more.
The bulge became expanded.
His food became demanded.
Until no one could stand it,
And now at this later date
He doesn't employ a plate.
For his indigestible mutton
The dear insatiable glutton
Preferring to munch it alone
With a hardy groan and a moan
Eats the shank including the bone.
While on a constant eating jag,
He bolts his food from a bag,
Which is made of heavy burlap,
And holds a glut which the chap
Puts down at a single sitting,
His manners worse than unfitting.

Elegy for a Squirrel in October

Luckless gray squirrel, laid out, crushed and dead,
Your life cut short neath an auto tire's tread,
No more playing with your sweet, Honey Bee;
For now lone to fare without you is she.
Your well hidden nuts from a season's hunts
Will be hard to find through long winter months,
And she'll need to find too another mate;
Your comforting presence in her leaf nest
She'll have no more when she's huddled to rest.
Writing this rhyme, myself I wouldn't hate,
If it hadn't been my tire and careless zest,
Which sealed forever that li'l creature's fate.

Mouse Trap

Till last month a mouse,
A wee tenant and friend
Lived in our farmhouse,
Where he met his end.
Not me nor my spouse
Nor anyone around
Had he ever harmed,
And with morsels found
He liked that we farmed.
Anyhow, a loud sound
One day had him alarmed,
And in a quandary
He hid in a dress
In the soiled laundry
Clothes hamper, no less.
Life can be mean!
I venture to guess
He just wasn't seen.
She threw the whole mess
In the washing machine,
Turned it on . . . yes,
So the light showed green.
Then in the process
Of becoming more lean,
Our friend died hapless,
Bedraggled and clean.

May

Scents of spring
Fill the air.
It's a time to sing
And a time to care.
It's time for a ring
On that finger there.
He'll be your king
And teddy bear.

Early March

A robin graced our birch today.
Spring's soon here, he stopped to say.
As winter songbirds disappear
Flying north until next year,
Springtime singers come along
To cure the silence with their song.
And others too who wintered south
Will soon return to river's mouth,
Neighboring marsh and fish filled lake.
The plain she-mallard with her drake
And long-necked gander with his goose,
Will join the otter, mink and moose,
For now ice from the lake is gone.
Thawed too is hoarfrost in the lawn.

Squirrels find nuts beneath nut trees,
Nuts they hid before the freeze,
And shedding now his coat, the hare
Begins to dress in summer wear.
Like we humans in our lives
Every other creature strives
To cope with winter's trials and aims
For milder spells when weather tames.
The wild March winds which howl and blow
Upsetting awning, trash and crow
Give way to calmer winds which bring
Bluebirds and robins singing, spring,
And new buds sprout from tree and earth,
As nature executes rebirth.

This winter has been, as of old,
Inside ennui, outside cold,
But warmer spells soon bring thaws,
A welcome end to winter blahs,
To sloppy slush, snow and sleet
With slippery ice beneath our feet.
No more frozen ears and noses,
Fingers, tears and tootsie toeses.
Spring will come, and when it does
Birds will sing and bees will buzz.

Its warmth and sweet, fragrant perfume
Will cure the world, I presume
Of all its suffering and woe.
Where will Old Man Winter go?

To Honey With Love

Whenever it rains,
I'm the nervous fella
With lumbar pains
And a black umbrella
Hurrying along
On the wet sidewalk
Without any song
And no time to talk.
If I happen to pass,
Don't stop at all.
Just step on the gas,
Don't whistle or call,
'Cause I'm occupied
With my aching back
And the hurt inside,
While sopping drops rack
My failing nerves
Which might be tested
By ladies' curves
Or else then bested
By the dire pain
That always nags
With pouring rain
And amorous hags
Who want of my time,
Some of my money
Or a flirting sign
And my umbrella, Honey,
Whenever it rains.

Clippings

I pruned our red geranium today,
Since a scad of deadwood had collected;
Some of its foliage had passed away,
Because its upkeep had been neglected,

But now its decline is over and done,
And it seems a very different plant,
Sits by the window in the noonday sun
With bright crimson flowers, however scant.

I think there are three or four, no more,
But enough to brighten our sheltered lives,
And there may be some new ones yet in store,
Because breathing freely the plant now thrives.

Without gangrene sapping life and vigor,
Its return to good health should escalate;
In about a month it should be bigger;
Yes, its prospects seem really, really great.

I had my own hair cut, and not for naught,
Seeing, it motivated this pruner,
Providing the boost which I had so sought.
I may flower too, if though, not sooner.

In the meantime I do feel much more whole;
A haircut, a shave, and I'm a new man.
Clippings can be good for a being's soul,
Be one an animal, plant or human.

Jexsuine Axial Hegxuzoide Cake or Stuma Cake

If you're having a party
Or wedding or wake,
Need something hearty,
That takes minutes to bake,
And can't think of a thing,
Don't make a mistake.
Tears of joy it may bring,
So for heaven's sake!
To have a real fling,
Just try hegxuzoid cake.

Base with old fetid cheese,.
Add in feathers of drake,
And pepper with bees
In the center a stake.
Frost it with grease,
To garnish a snake.
Mounted on fleece,
No imitation or fake
Is as certain to please
As jexsuine hegxuzoid cake.

Yes, to satiate a throng
With something you make
That'll last really long
And is made in a shake,
You just can't go wrong
For the time it will take.
Be a kitchen King Kong.
Although she may ache,
When you pinch that sarong
Tell her to serve piping hot pieces
Of jexsuine axial hegxuzoid cake.

To Whet Your Sense Of Humor

To whet your all too sober
And somber sense of humor,
Before you attempt a joke
Partake of a little toke.
Your mood will be much sunnier,
The joke will be much funnier.
I think I ought to know;
I have eaten enough crow,
Because quips I thought witty
Were considered a pity,
Because I just couldn't joke
At all without a toke.
Of course, there's also liquor
To make your humor sicker,
But if you would have a stroke,
Of genius you need that toke
Of merry marijuana.
Although you may not wanna
Allow yourself to divulge,
That you ever do indulge,
It will banish blues sooner
By bolstering your somber
And sober sense of humor.

Without You Near

To heck with cards
And people's regards.
I truly don't care
To play solitaire
And I'm lonely, dear,
Without you near.

The Gizzards, Papa Gizzard

All in all
I'm 'bout three feet tall.
That's exactly how high I grew,

And I'm twenty-nine,
Well past my prime.
My wife is twenty and through.

I'm pigeon-toed,
And one leg is bowed;
I wear an orthopedic shoe.

They say I'm a simp
Who walks with a limp
And is regarded as quite cuckoo.

My arms are long
And are super strong.
I can bend out the bars at the zoo.

My back is bent,
And my sense has went;
Say, Hello, I'll respond with: Goo!.

You can certainly see
The way that I be;
It's just horrible but all very true.

I cannot say
How I got this way;
It's such a shame to be so askew.

If it weren't for my pride,
I believe I'd hide,
And I ask now, wouldn't you too?

But I say with a grin,
I'm awry worse than sin.
Still, I want to be one of the crew,

And I'd like to be
Your cup of tea.
You see, I care so 'bout you.

The Gizzards, Mama Gizzard

I'd like to be
Your cup of tea,
So don't get mad and stew.

My hair is lost,
And my eyes are crossed.
I use close-up glasses, I do.

I wore a toupee
Till the other day,
The wind came up, and away it blew.

Because of that,
I wear a tight hat,
Which is like a sort of a kind of shoe.

The specs are bifocals
Made special for yokels
Who see things not really in view.

From working too hard
In the cattle yard,
I came down with a case of the flu.

I was nearly dead,
With some drink went to bed
And woke up in the morning dew.

I know I'm unique;
Even my beak
Is real odd, but it gets me through.

I get a bit drawn,
But I'm not all gone.
Made over I'm just like new.

I said I get drawn,
But I'm not all gone;
I'll get made over for you.

The Gizzards, Little Grensel Gizzard

Mom and Dad
Say I'm bad;
I've been this way, since I was two.

When I was three, about,
My teeth fell out,
But I don't got nothing to chew.

And often I drink
Like a running sink;
My sputum makes excellent glue.

Yes I imbibe.
You wanna know why?
It's because I can't put down the brew.

Now that I'm six,
I get my fix,
And voodoo I practice too.

And I'm a shade of green
You've never seen.
When I'm not green, I am blue.

But I wanna be
Your cup of tea,
In case you do need a clue.

Witch's Pitch

You needn't beware,
Because I'm not all there,
That I'm not though is probably true,

And supposing I'm square,
For sure I don't care;
For I'm kind of an egghead too,

But don't judge by my shape;
I should be a grape
Just from tippling so much brew.

If you've come to believe,
I have tricks up my sleeve,
It could be I'm somewhat like you,

And I'm sorry to say
My bod's in a way
A lot like a leathery shoe.

While the top of my head
Is a horn which is dead;
That's just the way that it grew,

And owing to that,
I can't wear a chic hat;
Only a dunce cap will do,

But if you want things spelled out,
Without question or doubt
My magic will always come through.

An Invocation For Trick-or-Treaters On Halloween

Jack-o'-lantern grinning mutely gold and bright,
Are you under some grim witch's binding spell,
And if you had your own tongue with which to smite,
What tales of horror and of madness might you tell,
Of tormented trolls and stalking skeletons, of ghouls
a- grave robbing?
Have you seen today a dead man dragging chain,
A black cat arched to the sound of someone's sobbing?
Hear that clinking and that grinding? What's that howl of pain?
Do you know the whereabouts of ghosts and goblins?
If aliens try to catch us, will someone take time to explain?
Are your spirit friends just waiting while in hiding
To make us wince and cower and die of awful fright?
And if we stray too far, will our parents be there chiding,
Or will we be snatched out this hallowed Halloween night?
Mr. jack-o'-lantern be our spirit friend in helping, guiding,
As we trick-or-treat after the end of today's daylight.

When There Were Ten

Zero was a hero,
But one put out the sun.
Two could tie a shoe,
As three climbed up a tree.
Then four opened a door,
While five jus t stayed alive,
And six was from the sticks,
But seven came from heaven.
Eight would fill your plate,
And nine walked up the line.
Now, then, there were ten.

Pilfering Blackberries

The world was my own, swell and swelteringly hot
And blackberries were big and ripe on their low-lying vines,
Where they impinged from an oak and scrub pine wooded lot
Upon the roadside in dog days of summertimes,
And sometimes between meals when I was a jaunty tot,
From our house I would cross the lawn, usually mowed,
And the infrequently traveled rural blacktop road
To find the dark rich beckoning berries, which yielded
To my small fingers from the rambling vines which wielded
Myriad teeny, keen thorns, till I had a handful
Of the fruit which amounted to a handy mouthful.
"No Trespassing" signs were for the most part unposted,
And my artless pilfering went mostly unnoticed
But for my ten telltale lavender besmirched fingers,
Which I would take home with no hat and no appetite.
Memory of those experiences to this day lingers,
Second only of such times to building a great kite,
Another theme on which I may hap one day to write.

Singtine Agen

Itz singtine agen
Co iber dum
Kal obic ferden
Kal ukul num

Per decker scit
Moo feedle fapper
Sunatai
sunatai
Fote neeper katin

Sunatai
Sunatai
sunatai
sunatai
sunatai

Bottle of Beer

Bottle of beer!
My ginger ale's here.
When I was a tyke,
Milk had no spike.
Now grown up,
It's another I sup.
Being a bit weak
And petite so to speak,
I was wanting for leverage,
So I made beer my beverage
And found at some length,
It gave me g reat strength,
So in lieu of other food,
I consume what's brewed.
If I get any older,
I'll try something bolder,
However just for now,
Especially when colder,
Not to bother a cow,
For fare that is golder
I'll sip my brewed chow.

Red Fred

Fred, Fred,
Your head's all red.
It's just as true,
That it isn't blue,
But every shred
Of the rest of you,
Not one bit blue
Is bright red too.
Had you cola instead
Of too much brew,
All the wrong med
And tainted stew,
You'd not be so red.
Regarding your head
And the bulk of you,
It needn't be said,
Red is better than blue.
But I think as I should
To be unduly lean,
It is understood,
With a pallor of green,
Wouldn't be good,
Having a bad spleen
And real sick in bed,
You're lucky, Fred,
Lucky you could
Be no worse than red,
Not blue or green
And not dead
And not seen.

Now As We Part

Girl of my dreams,
Apple of my eye,
It's not the way it seems
To you, saying good-bye,
For you're not aware,
As our parting is nigh,
That I always will care
And am loathe to show
You the pain that I feel,
This keen pain of dire woe
From a wound which won't heal,
Lest you would know,
And lest you should reel
From myself in despair,
For your lover's rapt heart
Has grown somber and spare.
Yet, it seems that we part,
Since you chose to aver
While off on a lark,
To one with an ear,
My sweet cherry tart,
That I hold you too dear.
Now I wait to embark
On a fast trip to jail.
Still, sing me that song
About jealous betrayal,
And tell me what's wrong
Till the sky grows pale.
They will pinch me ere long
Without tears or a fight.
I'll be busted and gone,
When the dawn gathers light.
Help your poor slave carry on,
Girl, I need you to love me tonight.

Sprout Of Luck

At that time of my life
Back in two thousand and four
Civil conflict was rife,
And I locked every door.

I had lost all my health,
Hair gone but for stubble.
And lacking fiscal stealth
Was in money trouble.

Without a single buck
And quite unemployable,
Bad and worsening luck
Was quite unenjoyable,

But one day while I mowed,
For a song a yard's sod
I unconsciously slowed;
As I'd seen something odd.

While I had chanced to gaze
O'er a lawn growing leaner,
My poor eyesight in ways
Became fleetingly keener,

I had spied a strange sprout
Off away a few feet;
Upon checking it out
My heart skipped a beat,

As I looked it over,
There, peeking pale green
Was a four-leaf clover,
The only one I've seen.

I chose not to reap it,
Thinking that the mother,
(Nor was I to keep it)
Just might spawn another.

.

Though my fortunate find
Was never repeated,
It imprinted my mind
Not to be deleted.

Mid grim hardships I'd found,
Against odds, that June day,
Lady Luck was around
To gift me in that way.

Notwithstanding the length
Of sweet time that She took
Before granting some strength
And the good goad to look,

At the end of my rope,
(For it had seemed just too late)
The wee sprout gave me hope
For an agreeable fate.

And with hope came vigor,
Plus the capacity
To be a tad bigger.
With generosity.

I opened a head shop.
Now with patrons galore,
I've found room at the top,
Impoverished no more.

Civil trouble is past,
And I'm liked in the hood.
With a toupee at last
I wear suits like I should.

Old strife recalled seems funny,
Good times were worth the wait.
With great luck and the money,
I'm a grateful thirty-eight.

And when the blues befall,
For I've seen but that one,
I'm obliged to recall,
That I might have seen none.

I think oft of less favored,
Who must cross from life over
Never once having savored
Sighting a four-leaf clover.

Robin's Breakfast

Something happened since the storm;
The grass and flowers amid;.
Robin Redbreast pulled a worm,
An elongated annelid
Which is a not so common term
For the quite common, squiggly worm..
He pulled it up is what he did
In getting breakfast in the morn
Instead of pouring flakes of corn.
Who complained? The katydid.

Maize After A March Storm, Raven And Me

In this rutted field of fallen cornstalks
An old, half blind and tattered raven walks,
Strutting about a splayed carcass of plant,
One of thousands that lie out flat or cant.

As though in mime of big longevous trees,
Withered stalks flitter in a constant breeze,
Which had turned about by early morning,
Following some of last night's fierce storming.

Besides the stiff breeze which dries the wet maize
Sun radiates its penetrating rays.
As if pierced with arrows, wry or prostrate
Evoking dying braves, the stalks dehydrate.

If they possessed as many vital nerves,
As the stalks do those, droopy long leaf curves,
Mightn't they flitter so without a wind?
Pondering such puzzles has my hair thinned;

Hair once naturally a corn silk gold
Seems, like the rest of me, to have grown old,
Having turned from blonde to roan, roan to gray,
Acquiring a deficit, one might say.

Since my scalp has a want of hair that way,
I hide what I have not with a toupee.
Concealing a crown which just grows more bald
Keeps doting friends from being more appalled.

About said puzzle, to hear just a word,
Could it make sense to hark to that black bird?
He would give voice, perhaps, to a crisp," Caw!"
Meaning yes, not, Gee! nor, however, Haw!

Goadings of Shiva or a warp of time,
Whatever it is that spurs on this rhyme,
Next strophe will be the one with which to stop;
That old black wraith just called me,"Carrottop!"

Hasn't that raven got some kind of nerve,
Showing such disrespect for my rare verve,
Advertising the fake red hair of mine,
To end an odd verse with this weird strophe nine.

Paroxysm

At noon one dog day in the park
We stopped to picnic on a lark
The heat had early reached a peak.
And later now, the sky looks bleak.
Dark thunderheads appear but thick,
Billows are getting inky quick,
The clouds churn in baleful gloom.
Underneath the world's a tomb.

The wind has waked turning leaves
And gradually more force achieves
It whips the bushes and the trees,
Is not an ordinary breeze
With haste we make it to the car,
Find out later we won't drive far.
That ill's afoot is evident
We head home with presentiment.

Suddenly bright lightning strikes,
As kids race home upon their bikes.
Tooting horns fracture the silence.
Slow people rush in compliance.
Ear-splitting thunder sometime late
Blasts, as we foresee ill fate
King-size raindrops begin to fall,
Splashing on and wetting all.

At length the storm proceeds to boil,
The clouds above in mad turmoil.
And all our fun and laughter cease,
As gale winds further still increase,
Windows shut as homes we pass.
People peer out at us aghast.
Like sails on passing boats, bent sheets
Of driving rain inundate the streets.

Visibility now all gone,
We stop beside a townie's lawn.
It really seems there'll be a flood;
There's danger too of sliding mud.
We hope the old dam doesn't fail,
As now fall ample rocks of hail.
They pelt the windows cracking glass
In vehicles; They quilt the grass.

Aged trees are felled through town
Bringing power lines straight down.
A giant chestnut topples near
Paralyzing each with fear.
Rain pours down till half-past five,
The road too swamped for us to drive
And as the storm starts to abate,
We see that damage there looks great.

Stopped we further check the site
And feel appalled, as well we might.
Mother Nature had had a fit
And wreaked revenge on us a bit.
We feel with death we've had a brush.
But for drips , there prevails a hush,
And to the east a rainbow shines
Above a village church and pines.

Exegetical

Cool and methodical calculations
Might reveal that the purport
Of outstanding sorts of disorder,
Barring some false connotations
Is akin to that of some sorts of order.
If between the two are just gradations,
Then surely it must be a relative matter,
And as chaos might be a phase of peace
From a quizzical point of view,
I'd like a piece of that chaos
To maybe start something new.

Some orders not kept within borders
Might cause mayhem or bedlam at best,
While disorder within when without
To its place might fall in and not out.

Though pondering the matter is surely no sin,
I don't like to presume or make guesses a lot.
Notwithstanding, at times I can't help but begin.
If you know of a good explanation, please, friend
Do tell it to me . . . Let me in!
One such escaped me, and now I am grieving,
But also I'm hounded by relative doubt;
And I can't stand the stress of believing,
It still needs in full to be figured out.

One Is Not Better Than Naught Or Than Two

There was a young toddler named Sue,
Who inexplicably lost a sole shoe,
A sole shoe of two shoes that were patiently wrought
And carefully picked out and lovingly bought
For Sue.
Now, remember this adage; it's true:
"Two shoes are better than one run down or new."
And I'm sure you can see as I do,
That for Sue a sole shoe was not better than two.
She thought, and she thought,
A sole shoe was her lot,
And you'll agree as you ought,
A sole shoe's worse than naught.
A sole shoe'd not be better for you,
Nor was a sole shoe any better for Sue,
A telltale sole shoe
With no mate in view,
No mate which was patiently wrought
And carefully picked out and lovingly bought,
One of two
For Sue.
A girl could be caught
With one shoe on and one not.
This affair and it's plot
Were proving bugaboo fraught.
What to do, what to do!
Boohoo-boohoo,
Boo hoo-boohoo !
She looked on top of the cot,
And she looked under the cot.
She sought and she sought
For the shoe they had bought,
And she looked in the other room too.
Her mom and her pa
Seeing she had but one shoe
Came to rescue
Poor Sue;
They checked every spot
In the house and the lot.
They checked the garage
From bottom to top.
They searched the whole kitchen through,
And the fruit of their search was no clue

As to how the sole shoe
Had vanished into the blue,
Till they eventually got
To checking a pot
Of boiling beef stew,
And submerged in the brew
Was the missing sole shoe.
Who would have thought
That the shoe of a tot
Brand new or not
Would be found in a pot
Of bubbling beef stew?
How could it ever have been true?
The enigma makes clear the bare basic fact
Which must ever be brought
Before others and pointedly taught and retaught,
That, shall I review:
Whether run down or not,
A sole shoe can never be better than none or than two
Be it black, white or brown, gold, red, purple or blue.

Posh

Fashioned by hand
A small birdhouse hangs
On a string from a limb.
One way then t'other
It turns in the wind,
And it swings.
A fool's invention, perhaps
But it shelters a nest;
For two bluebirds and young
It's the Ritz at its best.

So Long Indian Summer

Longer nights and shorter days are these.
Red, auburn, yellow-gold have left the trees.
And as the summer's songbirds now are gone,
Gone too are peepers piping dusk till dawn.
Flown with their flocks, the gander and the drake
Are far from ice that lies upon the lake.
The little junco, chickadee and thrush
Begin to frequent backyard, bush and brush.
And anointing pumpkins with its freezing dew,
Rime blesses too the vines on which they grew.
The field mouse in his den all snug and warm
Has made full ready for a gathering storm,
And as winter snow and sleet conspire to fly,
We must say to harvesttime...so long, good-bye,
And get cold weather's warmer vestures out,
Because that old man winter outside stalks about
Wanting much to nip your tender hands and ears
And bite those little tootsie toes, my dears.

To My Valentine

The truth I need you to know.
I'm tardy telling you, though,
Cherished, special valentine,
For I'm in love and I'm slow.

You should know you are fine
As precious perfume or wine,
And you ought to know too,
That I need you to be mine,

But you have nary a clue
About what's next to do,
When someone this beguiled
Wants to make it with you.

You're mild if though wild,
Unconstrained as a child.
Cupid, let fly your arrow,
For our Venus has smiled.

My love is of the marrow;
Don't leave me to sorrow.
This wooer's heart is true,
And will be so tomorrow.

Know, I live just for you;
Owing to you, I am blue.
I've cried many a sad tear,
Doubting you love me too,

So please draw to me here,
Whisper now in my ear.
Tell me you love me, dear,
And you'll always be near.

All Is Fair

A fair and worldly lady, happily betrothed
Looked really good to me, theretofore unloathed.
Another suitor's sweetheart-wife to be was she,
But I told her self-assuredly to court with only me.
She, a girl full wise to wants and ways of men
Chose not to shun me quickly there and then
But to pluck each taut and tender string
Of my naïve and wanton heart and improvise
A discomposing game of love which would bring
To me an unexpected and enduring harsh demise.
She plucked and played each day and night,
Until my heartstrings tore and broke,
But I know now, it was fair and right
That she should toy that way and poke
Coquettish fun at me, a would-be thief;
My covetous love was but to her a tired joke.
Was her fiancée her heart's delight, her friend and chief?
Many a year it took to mend my hurt and assuage my grief.

October Rain

for Sergeant Major T.
and others who have died

Disconsolate, October rain
Pummels with drops my window pane
And keeps me pent, alone inside
This lorn house, where I'm occupied
With dreary thoughts now here again.

Still, in this lonely place I'll bide,
Until that time when I'll have died.
Beat, rain, against my window glass,
And down without, for you will pass,
As sorrows pass, when I have cried.

My crying, though, befits not class;
I want to not again be crass,
But just to spend this lonesome time
Scrawling down a bittersweet rhyme
Betwixt looks through my pane at grass.

But, while I'm loath to sob and whine,
I, nonetheless, can't help but pine,
As over wet lawn grass blades gleam,
And through blurred glass educing theme;
Each captured glimpse spurs too a line.

When too, of other times I dream,
Of bygone days and nights which seem
To have bestowed on me rare dears
To whom (who live) I'm in arrears
With letters penned, as dears can deem.

Alas, the grass is soaked with tears
All spilled o'er missing kin and peers;
It's when thus anguished storm clouds bawl,
As with their sorrowing drops fall,
For loved are dead, some short of years.

And yes, dead loved ones I recall,
Held fast to hopes that were not small,
They smiled kind smiles which quelled dour fears.
Brave souls with whom I toasted: "cheers!"
Are, in mine heart, not dead . . . at all.

Warning To An Earthworm

Slippery Earthworm, pink and brown
Alayin' stretched out 'twixt the grass,
Who came up out upon the ground
Under a solstice moon to bask,
Before the break of early day
You'd better slip back on down in
Or as a tasty breakfast pay
A hungry Mr. Red Robin.

Dependable Friend

I have a good friend who is the dependable type
And is the image of well-being, fullness and strength,
Who's not swayed by opinion or gossip or hype,
And who I look to and like to study at length.
Let me cite in a way to clearly characterize:
He's a pet and a pal in a pot, a geranium,
Who helps me often, my thoughts to better organize,
Banishes nervous tension and relieves tedium
He likes to grow, blossom and photosynthesize,
Was purchased for free but holds a high premium.
The tint in his blossoms is like the pink florid flush
In the face of a teenager exposed with a crush.
My friend's foliage looks like profiles of trumpets.
Then too, his leaves look a lot like little lily pads.
He's there when we others share hot tea and crumpets
And actively discuss life's goods and its bads,
Sans words from my pal churlish or argumentative.
Of qualities like patience he's quite representative.
I can talk to him, and he doesn't talk back to me,
Always there for my solace, he turns not his back on me,
Would never our friendship give away, sell or barter,
And asks for naught but occasional drinks of water.
I know sometime, days must end for my geranium.
When that time comes, I trust I'll be able to take it,
For 'twill just have to be, with perhaps a small requiem.
In the meantime my bosom friend helps me to make it.

We Build Us A Kite

To dispel depression,
And bring some delight,
To make an impression,
We'll build us a kite,
Then sail it some later,
When the wind is right.
First we cut the paper,
Paper and sticks,
String it to caper,
Swoop and do tricks.
To make it ride steady,
A tail we will fix,
And with that it's ready,

A wondrous fling,
To enter the sky
The clever thing,
Rises up high
On a very long string
Beneath the clouds
And sometimes above,
Awes the crowds;
It's a great paper dove
Or eagle or hawk,
And a labor of love,
The cause of much talk.
We built us a kite.

Autumn's Gold

From summer's heat, timely fall reprieves,
Then quilts the land with multicolored leaves.
Now that we're getting on past October,
Some leafs dot trees that leaves had cloaked over.
Like holiday seasons which soon have passed,
The fall beauty doesn't a long time last.
Colored carpet, earth's terrain is a scene
Of yellow, red, brown and remnants of green.
But for some stragglers, trees show an absence
Of the leaves which now blanket the earth whence
Sprang elms, oaks and other genres which are
Loosing windblown leaves which fly near and far.

Defying the want for relevancy,
Like trinkets left up on each yuletide tree,
Some hanger-on leaves seem fancy to be.
As trees spend the last of their scanty dress
To gild the earth's sod and its boundlessness
A leaf singly detaches itself... yes
With an instance of inaudible sound,
If caught by the wind, may fly all around,
Then fall down to join the wealth on the ground
Where frozen the winter long it may stay
Then thaw out in spring and later decay,
Enriching earth's soil in that wonted way.

But when coldhearted winter proceeds to freeze
You start to yearn for the month of May...please,
The cold can impact the way a soul sees:
Looking like giant blood vessel bouquets,
Stark against skies of diaphanous days,
Trees bare of leaves abide as winter flays
Them with sleet, snow and ice mid low degrees,
But all that, they shrug off, and then to tease
The cold season they go soundly to sleep,
Till the promise of spring they wake to keep.
They play a part in the rebirth foretold,
Bursting new leaves, which, we later behold
Gracing the hillsides as autumn's rich gold.

What Doesn't Always Happen On A Homeless Winter Day

At the break of day
You couldn't sleep the whole night,
And you rise up from the hay
With no real rest in sight.
Helter-skelter,
Out of the shelter.
Lovely morning, (minus-nine)
To wait in the local soup line.
Under foot it's glare ice.
You slip and fall to grovel twice
While trekking over ten thousand feet
To the long line for a beggar's treat.
Then, you're told to stand and wait
Till a quarter after or half past eight,
And you're getting frost bit frozen toes
As fiercely now it snows and blows.
At nine o'clock or quarter past
The soup kitchen door is unlatched at last,
And it's said through a very narrow crack,
"There's an apparent dreadful shortage-lack.
It'll be just bread and cold oat cereal."
Which seems to be not immaterial.
But for starvation
And needing to beat it,
You'd pass up the ration,
Yet you manage to eat it.
Around mid-morning
Along the icy sidewalk
Your given a warning,
As two city cops talk.
"Keep on trucking!"
You're rudely told,
And you know you're not lucking
Though seventy years old.
You stop at the library,
There to delve,
Till you hear,"Don't tarry!"
A little past twelve.
At mid-afternoon
Arrives a tad of help,
And none too soon

Sandwiches are dealt
By an inner city gospel group,
And gratitude is felt,
'Cause there's also warming soup.

The rest of the day
In seedy fashion
You while away
At the train station,
And you start to think
About your situation,
That you'd like to have a drink;
And there you sort of lounge
Till after seven-thirty
Unable to scrounge
The price, you're so dirty,
So you walk to the shelter
Just a little bit late.
It's getting colder,
And there you wait,
Someone getting older,
As they lock the gate.

Verbena

It seems an awful pity,
And I ask for your pardon,
But you're very much too pretty
To be in my flower garden.

Verbena, purple-blue,
Sweet Verbena so petite,
Though others are lovely too,
With you they can't compete.

Like sprays of wild violets
Having centers all of white
Your wreaths of wee florets
Hint of the deepest night,

Shinning out, it seems,
Wee keen beacons bright
Like heavenly beams
Of incandescent light.

I would you were a woman;
You'd have me all aglow.
With your sweet allurement
You'd steal a beauty show.

Weight of Winsome Winter

How the winter winds do blow
The frigid, driven sleet and snow
With nary a sign of slowing,
And attitudes just hatch and grow.

Risky is the sidewalk going
Riskier still to drive, I'm knowing.
As degrees drop off, I'm supposin',
That my car's in need of towing

But find myself among the chosen
To be bent over stiff and frozen,
As I check beneath the hood
Which on my backside keeps on closin'.

When the car starts, like it should,
That petrol's low is understood.
I need more fuel with zero bread,
Yet, find my credit card's still good.

While driving home to go to bed;
I really have to use my head.
The engine wants to skip and gun;
Along the road my car's a sled.

I try not to dream a lot of sun,
Hope where children skate and run,
Lake ice this year is not too thin,
So that the kids can have safe fun.

My car's condition now's a sin;
I'll need one still to transport kin,
And cars are just too steep to buy,
Albeit I'd trade the old one in.

Petroleum costs are now so high,
That fuel prices seem to reach the sky,
While earnings touch an all-time low.
And trying to plan, I want to cry.

Of bills I can't just stop the flow,
Fiscal repair is much too slow,
And winter months can weigh...I know;
I live in New England where it's so.

Under a Winter's Topsy-Turvy Spell

for Archie:
a pet crow
who died

Myriad crows' tracks I spy in the snow.
Where did their makers come from,
And where, now they're gone, did they go?
In aggregates of aggrandized crows' feet upside down,
The legs reaching up, each from a giant half interred crow,
They have become the trees all bare now since autumn.
The ash trees, maples, chestnuts and oaks which show
Themselves extending upward from the near horizon
Are silhouetted against the evening's dim afterglow,
Crows' feet upended and embodied in those tree branches.
Capriciously in breezes dance upside down dances.

Crock

I own a small crock
For sick-pills, quite a few;
I call it Dr. Spock;
It holds other stuff too,

Like a clean handkerchief
To dry my wet knees,
Wet from tears of grief;
Copious are these.

When they begin to well,
And pour down past my shirt,
You can certainly tell,
That my feelings are hurt.

And on account of that
Humiliation seen,
(Keep it under your hat.)
A reputation I glean

With my own local crowd.
I get emotional, see,
And I cry awful loud.
Now, wouldn't you be

Kind of emotional too,
If your favorite crock,
Polka dotted and blue,
Cracked on a big rock?

I slipped and let go of it.
Loosing my grip, it just fell.
Because of a conniption fit.
It was the end, I do tell.

As it dropped like a stone.
Raucously I bawled,
Though I was quite alone,
I squalled and I squalled

Turquoise was its hue
With polka dots all neat.
And practically new,
It just cracked at my feet.

Once again come the tears.
Out with a handkerchief.
Drat the darn local peers...
Polka dots of gold leaf!

I wailed quite out loud,
And discarding my attire,
I donned a red shroud,
Shinnied up a church spire,

And signaled a chum
With my red shroud on fire.
The rain doused it some,
As I climbed up higher,

Not to be a clown,
Since I might have tried flying,
I had to climb down,
And terminate my crying.

Now from this loopy rhyme,
To repair my blue jar,
I'll take out some time
.At this private brew bar.

Forgetting milk and sloth,
(I was so wrong to mix them.)
And given time and cloth,
We will glue cracks to fix them.

Though the crock's split in three.
We'll wrap it with silk,
After applying glue, see!
So much for spilt milk.

And I know you will find;
If we just wait right here
That the good glue will bind,
While we have some more beer,

And coming out like new,
The crock is soon mended.
We were able to make do;
On which note Crock's ended.

For Sons And Daughters On Mothers' Day

Hip-hip-hooray!
Hip-hip-hooray!
For all of our mothers
On Mothers' Day.

If it's one or another
Directive you need
For treating your mother
On her day in deed,

Here's some advice
Time-tested to do.
Without guise or device
It follows for you:

Bring her fresh flowers,
Cultivated or wild,
Those mood elevators
Fragrant and mild.

Buy her a gift
And a lovely card
With an apropos script
By a talented bard.

Cook her a meal,
Breakfast in bed;
Compel her to feel
Like a newly wed.

Read her the paper
Let her relax.
Discuss the news after;
Have fun with the facts.

Put on some music,
Something she'll like,
Country, rap, classic
Or some other type.

Finish the housework;
Clean all and the sink.
Don't fail to uncork
And pour her favorite drink.

Give her your time,
If she wants to talk.
Ask her: Is she fine?
Take her for a walk.

If all of this little
You just cannot do,
I'll bet that she'll settle
For less since it's you.

Still and yet touch her day
With the happiness of May,
And before the day's through,
Kiss her thrice nicely, you.

For St. Paddy's Day, A Corny Hat

In queues vivid green plants
Get the rain, the sun and ants.
To copy grander, older trees,
They shake so gently in a breeze.
Oblong ears mid loopy shoots
Quaver on stalks above wry roots.
If endowed as much with nerves,
As is maize with verdant curves,
It just might shake so sans all wind.
! !
! !
With stress from such discernments my off-white hair has thinned.

The Old Carpet

It lasted many a year, and enchanting the sight,
A rich feast for the eye upon opening a door
Or seen in the evening bathed in warm lamplight
Its colors hinted of far off places and their lore,
A battlefield for toy soldiers with their conjured might,
For the dog and cat to rest, it cushioned the hard floor.
Providing mice with their own, private playground at night,
It's been a doormat to rid shoes of dirt, grit and more.

It was the pride of the people who had it laid there,
Though its lavish presentability now is gone,
With a now departed era of statusy flair
When the motif that guests would party and dance on,
Seemed more foreignly fresh, ineffable and rare,
For kids it was a surface to play, romp and prance on,
A large, exotic rug to cover floorboards elsewise bare,
But its patterned design has become faded and wan.

The living room carpet's no good, one often now hears,
For it has grown dilapidated, tattered and worn.
While serving a long lifetime of arduous years,
It has generated holes; its threadbare edges are torn,
All soiled by scuffed drippings and the spillings of beers,
So sullied it won't do for just one more gala bash.
As the end of its utility rapidly nears,
It's too decrepit to clean and must go with the trash.

Once the unique embodiment of beauty and grace,
Which drew often together close friends, kin and peers,
Lending a grand ambience to the living room space,
It's been the site of many a hearty toast of: "cheers!"
Soon to disappear but for memories without a trace,
As it's rolled up and dropped by the curb with some tears,
And another new and lovely is put in its place
To captivate and to comfort in ensuing years.

Maple Syrup

Grand old sugar maple tree,
In whose sanctum I like to be,
Out of the dull world, where I climb,
Here in your limbs I love to rhyme.
With gratitude to you I cling,
As of your fortitude I sing.
Whether in daylight or by moonlight
From far away or nigh, your sight
Awakens in my spirit's core,
A keen yearning to know you more.
When feral animal and fowl,
Squirrel, chipmunk, jay and owl
In hot weather, cold or warm
Are in your keeping through storm,
When maple sap buckets appear
Upon your trunk that time of year,
And as the winter takes its leave
Granting another year's reprieve,
Or as you bud new leaves in spring,
Of your loveliness I sing.
When changing with the fleeting scene,
You turn a deeper shade of green,
And as I whistle a happy tune,
Because we're getting into June,
Then like a sovran priest or priestess
You preside o'er woods at solstice,
And with the summer's risen heat
Which everybody needs to beat,
You grant sweet refuge from the sun.
When you're a jungle gym for fun,
Or when a strong bough holds a swing
On which rocks glad a child, I sing.
When in turning leaves you're dressed,
During the time of fall harvest,
The least of your magic to make
Would a flock of witches take;
You paint yourself without a brush
In many colors crisp and lush,
Orange, gold and amber red,
Then, in bleak winter months play dead,
As window panes white with rime lace,
And a fire burns in each fireplace

Stoked with the deadwood brisk wind trims,
And sticks and logs from your spent limbs.
When in creating a royal show,
You deck yourself with sculpted snow,
And while you're a capricious thing.
It's of your loveliness I sing.
Lumbered after your course is run,
When your prevailing days are done,
At last decayed or felled you fall,
For then the axman pays a call.
He doesn't really care at all,
Nor does he ever laze, you know
Since, everybody has to go.
I shed no tear, but just cheer up,
And have a treat with maple syrup,
For you will live long after I
Have met my end, said my good-bye,
And with regard to woes meanwhile,
I can but pleasurably smile.
Within your limbs, under your wing,
Of sweet security I sing.
A bigger, older friend to me,
I'll again tell you, maple tree.
You'll wave your limbs like angels' wands,
To indicate: "We've common bonds."
And with a breeze you'll breathe a sigh
Which says, "You are; so too am I."

A Fish To Be Caught

Poor boy at town's end,
Don't think you can't win.
Find a stick for a pole,
A stick long and thin.
With a rock for a spade
And a can made of tin
Dig up wiggly worms
Which are slippery as sin.
On a line that is string
Bait a hook that's a pin.
Just like you were taught.
Not any time soon
Can such tackle be bought.
Take it all to the glen;
The fish which you've sought
Is in the creek's bend
And is there to be caught,
So to your fishing go tend.
With the patience you've got
You'll catch the fish, and you'll win.

Salute To The U.S.

I hear that trouble brews
Across the sea,
And I give thanks the news
Ain't ‘bout me.
Yes, I am blessed with a roof and board
And much security,
No pain of want, no need to ward
Off uncalled for enmity.
My acquaintances all are friends,
Not anyone an enemy,
As we share life's dividends,
And, yes, we all are free.

A Rhyme of Bobby B. Blue

They call me Bobby B. Blue who knows just what to do
I dwell within reach,
This is the way that I preach
Though ofttimes in the pulpit, I'd sooner be in a pew.
I don't want to be bold,
If you need to be told,
But let this be something to chew:
You're not just tripe
Whatever your type,
The thought is for you, and is true.
If you're really good looking,
Tend to you're cooking;
Admirers and rivals can cause a to-do.
And if you don't take a prize
On account of your size,
Don't think you're not one of the crew.
If you're the least bit gigantic,
Never be frantic;
There's plenty of room for all of you.
Plus your bigness is treasure.
Your strength beyond measure,
Too, you might have more room for some brew.
If you're real, real little,
You can bow a wee fiddle
To scold at night like a shrew.
When you're too tired to roam
And want to stay home,
Just take up abode in a shoe,
But if neither little nor big,
Don't give a good fig;
It's just the way that you grew.
That is; if you happen to be
Plain and ordinary,
Dry your vain tears and be yourself, you.
When you throw a party,
Don't be a smarty;
Invite kith and kin, but some new people, do.
Upon entering society,
Lend your variety;
Something maybe needed by and from you too
And there could be at some point
Some fun in sharing a joint,

But when everyone wants a real hullabaloo,
It can take a lot
Of expensive pot
To make mundane, old things seem new,
And once in a while,
Laugh, weep or smile,
One must accept this, don't stew:
Whether hippie or sot,
If you smoke too much pot
Though you try to be wise while true-blue,
And though you come from good stock,
You could befriend an odd clock
Which will say and will drive you, "cuckoo".
Whatever our sort,
Stick-in-the-mud or sport,
These facts are meant for me and for you,
And it makes good sense
To give thought to the tense,
While maintaining an overall, eternal view,
As we hypothesize
And ponder past lives
Deep in thought in a house, an old cave or igloo
So as to know how much
We were really in touch
Before some of our lifetimes were through.
And it may have been
That we were in sin,
So we think and pray about what we should do,
And we say there's no way
We would ever slay
No way ever, though in wartime we slew
So it might be but right
To be contrite,
Be we Buddhist, other heathen, Christian, or Jew.
We're yet all together
With or without tie or tether,
Birds of many a feather who rose up and flew.
When another time,
We have occasion to rhyme,
We'll just have to toast with a glass or two,
But as for now,
May it be that somehow,
This verse has galvanized who's concerned, if just a few.

Missing You

I need you in the evening
When shadow from the hill
Spreads its velvet covering
Across the sunken dell.

And I need you in the morning;
I need you in the daily light,
But I love you best at gloaming,
When the day melts into night.

It's then your presence fills me
With unspeakable desire,
And then your sweet love thrills me,
As you set my soul on fire.

I wish we were together.
Yes, I wish that you were near.
I guess, you're with some other,
And how I miss you, dear.

Souvenirs

On a rainy day like today
I find my mind has gone astray
To other times and other places,
To friends I had and have no more;
Having gone they left few traces
Save for the memories that I adore.
Such days are made for recollection,
Riffling through old cards and letters
And an inscrutably strange selection
Of antique relics and attention getters:
Shards of silver driftwood, dried chestnut,
An eagle's quill,scallop shell, red oak acorn,
A little book from a deserted hermit's hut
And a lock of hair from a lover's shock shorn,
Showing a praying figure, a blessed photo cut,
Hand carved buttons from a jacket once worn,
A drawing of a wrestler with an extra large gut,
And two black armbands with which to mourn
Are some of the treasured, sentimental souvenirs
That, so displayed , my bedroom shelves adorn,
Ever to evoke happy smiles or melancholy tears,
And other emotional signs and symptoms, born
Of sweet nostalgia for the fond and former years,
And every now and then I have another brain storm.
To keep my memory green and impress puzzled peers
I add another curio attempting to not meet the norm
For pack rat behavior which my habituation often nears.

The Common Dandelion

They say the poor dandelion
Is nothing but a useless weed.
Yet it can cheer up a dull lawn
Blossoming or going to seed.

A throng of the blooms just might
Gladden the saddened lad or lass,
As if bright stars from the deep of night
Dotted a yonder of verdant grass,

And when parboiled in a pot
Or fresh in a salad with beans,
Naught can please a whole lot
Like lowly dandelion greens,

As nothing in this world is
More exceedingly fine
Than a cup or a chalice
Of dandelion wine,

So if in your own opinion
Your personal virtues are scant,
And you feel you're just too common,
Remember the commonplace plant.

If I Were An Elf

If in this wide, wide world I were a little elf,
I'd state my purpose plain and wouldn't hide
Behind another's back, nor a door all by myself,
Making sure in my mind and heart, that I was bona fide,
For otherwise I could find myself right up a big old tree.
I'd walk the straight and narrow path noting too the wide,
Doing that which was required to carry on with liberty,
And in such ways as these I would prevail and would abide.
If someone twice my size and strength were to challenge me,
While on tippy toes I stood beneath that person's belt,
I'd wisely tell him that he really didn't have a plea,
If that was as a rule the way he thought and felt,
I'd have him sit, and then I'd hop onto his king-size knee,
And I would ask him if before nobility he'd ever knelt.
Then with care I'd fix for him a piping pot of green herb tea
Putting him at ease, till his cold, hard heart began to melt,
Then I'd tell him that the light he needed much to see,
And that for now he needn't eat another little smelt,
That, if I were he, I would prefer instead some tripe,
As with tiny paper planes his great body I'd pelt.
And then I'd ask real cool like, if he were the type
To think my wee airplanes could bring a single welt.
I'd tell him that I'd recommend for him a ranking stripe,
Before asking, did he not think this poem dumb and trite?
And if he wept at that question, his tears I'd sadly wipe,
Until he answered kind of slow and with an air polite,
"While tripe and smelts are nice, I'd rather have a snipe."
And said, "It's really nice, you know, to have a proper light,"
As he'd wait patiently and smile, and have me light his pipe,
Then smoke and smoke so as not to lose it all nor get uptight,
And now, that he could handle tasks demanding greater size,
I'd sense, and since I'm lacking when it comes to might,
Although he were not quick of mind, clever nor wise,
I'd find, that he could help me with his weight and height,
And I'd convince him that he was to me one of the guys,
And that to make peace with me it was ne'er too late.
I'd bake and serve to him some fresh blueberry pies
And him I'd truly try to please and wouldn't hate.
Then knowing that our kinship now was on the rise.
I'd ask him just to hold a ladder high and straight,
So that it penetrated outer space past earthly skies,
Since we needed now to find the sacred pearly gate.

And then, before explaining whens and hows and whys,
I'd climb right up there for the both of us, my little self
To bring back down what each of us had dire need of,
If I had to steal it off of the Great Almighty's shelf.
I'd embrace him who was the bigger, taking heed of
The one who put me in this world to be an elf.

Afflicted Some

Through the grapevine I've heard
I'm considered a nerd,
And some say I'm also a sleaze.

I have a girl
Who likes to purl.
She's just such a terrible tease.

I sleep in the weeds,
Where the wild thing breeds,
And I've made some friends who are fleas.

Hold your nose,
If you get near my toes.
My feet smell a lot like cheese.

I have a cough
Which ticks me off,
And also, I frequently sneeze.

When I don't do those things,
No pleasure it brings.
The rest of the time I just wheeze.

There's just no way
Except to pray
To be cured of this awful disease.

I'm as blind as a bat
And aloof like a cat,.
It's mostly myself I aim to please.

Down in the dumps,
In one of my slumps,
I can't see the forest for the trees.

I'm really a doll,
Who likes to crawl,
But I spend too much time on my knees.

I'm trying hard
To be a bard,
But I'm finding, that it's no breeze.

I'm growing older
And it's getting colder.
I'm just so afraid, that I'll freeze.

When all is said and done,
I'm afflicted some,
But my troubles could be worse than these.

Poems by Family and Friends

It's So Hard

By Christopher Braithwaite
For His Mother, Dorothy A. Wilkerson

It's so hard when you leave and your heart is scared
It's so hard
When you got that last card
Knowing you have a friend somewhere
And you know you're no longer near
It's so hard
Knowing this is the last
And these days move fast
It's so hard
Yet I shed my tears
And no one is near
It's so hard
Giving, something and someone takes back
It's so hard
I never lack the stress
Knowing I was given the best
I know my fears but I thought no one cares
It's so hard

Midnight

By Dorothy A. Wilkerson

Midnight's tunes passed through many back doors
walked over the thresholds of pain,
midnight, scorned, appeared like a Shakespeare drama
where tragedy and joy played hand and hand
when the back door was the way
the dark threshold was crossed
midnight's tune played on midnight's tune played
the city streets, where candle light danced to midnight's tune,
candle light danced where crimson shadows celebrate,
Midnight's shadow fell and played to a world
on crimson streets. Let's celebrate

Neon Love

By Dorothy A. Wilkerson

Warm beneath your feet silky to the touch
you sat gazing into the dream that followed you
through the color of dreams and neon love.
Even I loved the color of neon love
I love the way you love embracing time,
sitting by the water that waltzed by,
Yes, I love the way you love loving the laughter
dancing city lights against the night time sky,
loving how you loved the rhythm of the city beat
nights of dancing feet places filled with a laughter
music that lifted the heart even then I loved you,
you who traveled into the path of political storms
that became a season of unrest,
even that stormy path couldn't change the color of neon love,
yes I love the ways of your love,
even then you knew some day that love would be you.

Speak

By Dorothy A. Wilkerson

An old tune, a mellow song
Took us back, back
To a time that stood still for us, even if only for a short while, a time…
When the world danced to old songs,
A time when harmony fell like rain drops, each a ripple of melodic notes
Humming, a tune that set the feet to dance
That certain something, that feel good feeling
Made love come alive, giving the spirit something,
loving that speaks and lives
The spirit spoke a language of its own
And it plays on...

The Covering

By Dorothy A. Wilkerson

Even when energy flows and rushes like the tide,
You cover me
Your water fills me, and I overflow like a stormy sea
Yet you cover me
I have my being in you, and you in me,
And I rise and flow
Like the tide
you lift me up
In you I breathe I
You cover me

Blue Skies

By Charlaine Taylor

On a day like today
There must be a way
For things to end happily ever after,
But this just calls for laughter.
There's no way that can be
That all ends so prettily.
Give up on all that.
It all seems subsumed.
In the thought that's assumed
The moment's enough
Forget that other stuff
Because dreams can't come true.
Make the moment enough for you.

Child With Pink Petunias

By Charlaine Taylor

The child walks around the borders of the garden.
Again and again she circles the pink flowers.
She breathes in their fragrance so many times over.
These are the things that this little child will live for.

In the middle of the farmyard, the squared wire fence
Is topped with barbed wire to keep all things in or out.
She stoops down low to see, and reaches out to touch
Such brief beauty centered in the bustling farm life.

She knows that none of this can possibly be hers,
But still she bends and admires all this profusion:
The transience of pink loveliness surrounding her;
The passing moment of wonder at things in bloom.

The child wears a plain, colorless, flowery dress,
That falls about her knees and thighs, enclosing them.
She has on anklets and black, patent leather shoes,
That attach her to the grassy ground she stands on.

Easter Poem

By Charlaine Taylor

Baskets trimmed and filled and tied
With a bow. Pink, yellow, blue
Eggs and a chocolate bunny to reside
In green grass; waiting just for you.

Marshmallow chickens hatching too.
Spring apparel, hair styled, all is new.
What more do you need, and what do you do?
The countryside renews itself just like you.

Easter morning; to church you go.
You leave and then, turning, you go back in.
What did you leave behind? You know.
Your umbrella. What a way to begin.

All is not perfect. The sky's filled with rain.
Did you forget the meaning? Add
All of the above. Turn and go out again.
Remember: Do not forget the sad

Event leading up to the glad, new
Rebirth, the happiest you've ever had.
Celebrate. Count your blessings, and you
Remember the good t hat came after the bad:

That from darkest winters, always comes Spring.
The first Easter morning, gone from the tomb,
But still with you. Recall, rejoice and sing,
The shining glory that came from the
sad cross's gloom.

Endings

By Charlaine Taylor

Floating gentle on the breeze of fall,
Closing curtains on summer's springing,
Down falling down, the days of summer,
Summer's songbirds and summer's laughter
Ending, gone and leaving memory.
So, now the year is full of waiting
Till our summer once more comes again.
Brief summer sets the stage with flowers,
Now blossoming with all things growing,
Rays of light flowing on shades of noon.
Shadows increasing, as light dims down.
Enter autumn that precedes winter.
Quick passing are the days of lively
Warmth, bending, shining, bowing to fall.

Entrance

By Charlaine Taylor

In a towel he stood there.
A towel was all he wore.
In the doorway; all bare
But one towel and nothing more.
She closed the car door and up the walk
She started. How could they talk?
Up the front steps...across the porch too.
She had no idea of what she'd do.
He opened the screen door too.
She didn't know a single thing
But she knew he knew
What this would bring.
"How, why, when and where."
She thought. He had a complacent air,
And the towel was spotless and white.
Yes, this would take the night.
This small towel changed everything.
If she entered, then what would that bring?
"I've been playing handball."
He said. "Come on . Come in."
He looked in her eyes with a grin
And pushed the door wider and took her hand.
"Enter." He stood watching her. She
Didn't know what to do. But he
He of course exactly precisely knew.
He smiled, and this was nothing new.
He was in command. What could she do?
This would change everything. So
She'd regret her decision to come or to go.
For the rest of her life, and more.
The towel seemed smaller, whiter, the door
Seemed wider. She knew she had to grieve.
But he reached for her, to receive
What she held in her hand,
And that's when she knew he'd understand.

For A Poet

By Charlaine Taylor

Because there was no one else but you,
Because there was no one else to go to,
I went and wondered if you at all knew,
That this was really why I came to you.

I at times wondered if you could have guessed
That you were there, and I was there, at best.
And that was all that brought us together
We were both storm tossed much like the weather.

This is just what I want you to believe.
I now have reasons to wish to deceive.
I, of course, was the first one to leave.
All that you had you gave me to achieve.

You also gave me all of your passion.
We were true to the best of our fashion.
You said you'd be walking down thc hallway,
So I never thought then, that you would stay.

Giving It Up

For Robert Frost

By Charlaine Taylor

She is trying to have it all
She is beautiful: large, dark eyes,
Sculpted face, an eighteen inch waist.
And "The lovely shall be choosers."

She is twenty-one years old,
When decision time comes to her.
She knows it. There are two choices.
Two paths diverge in her short life.

She knows she only has one chance.
She's sure she can never change this.
Her life can never be the same.
There's no retracing her footsteps,

No going back ever again,
She can't get off a plane or train
And turn around, run back again,
Because the place will be different.

This very place will not be there.
She can only look from afar
To see where she once could have been.
To recognize the one she once was,

And the one she will be no more,
But she turns and makes the wrong choice.
She quite simply takes the wrong path.
Nothing will ever be the same.

She can't turn around, start over.
She can't make up her mind to change.
There is no turning back for her.
All she can do is remember.

Too late the time has come and gone.
Before she loses everything,
Turn around, turn around, go back.
There's not another chance for her.

Mothers' Day Poem

By Charlaine Taylor and Robert Olmsted

Within the deepest slumber, calm and mild as night,
A joy just to remember, shinning ever bright
And often the hardest one about whom to write
Is the one who always always loves you best,
Singing in the quiet hours sacred to the blest,
Riding on the sweetest dreams' swaying, singing crest.
Hard is the song it sings.

Hard is the trial it brings.
Hard in everything is simply to be mother,
However, she can love you quite like no other,
Though, hard it is to know for what a child cries out,
And that to know beyond the shadow of a doubt,
So as to have her caring meet the child's own need,
Something in which she always does somehow succeed.

Poem In July

By Charlaine Taylor

I am a book. Open me wide.
See inside of me: wide, wider.
Hold me gently. Turn my pages.
Now you can turn all my pages,
You see. Just look at them flutter,
With the touch of your fingertips.
Read me. Do you know my story?
Move slowly and with tenderness.
Wide, wider, hold me in your hands.
You have seen more than my cover.
Now, do you want to go further?
Oh, the wonders I can show you.
They are all here waiting for you
In words that express all to you.
If you close me, all that I am
Will fold softly, so silently,
Having never been read at all,
Never to be touched as before.
You would never know my story.
If you will only open me,
This is why I was created.

One Way Of Looking At A Blackbird

By Charlaine Taylor

Yesterday was spring, then summer
Then the crow caws, caw, like that.
Nothing to crow about, caw, again
High and shrill and sharp, caw cuts
And circles through gray light. Blackbird
Flies by, sees a scarecrow, lights
On a line and perches there, caws.
This then is the first of fall, the
Beginning, falling down into
Long winter. Caw, cloying, sharp,
Harsh sound: sounding the colding
Air, cutting, stabbing through the gray
Skies graying into the guise of
Slanted sunlight, lighting barely
Enough. The encroaching fast
Falling cold to colder to coldest
Approaches. Here the blackbird comes
Where there is little more warmth
In the last diminishing light.
The dark cries pierce the icy soul.
This bird is the herald of freeze,
Filling darkness with its blackness.

The Hope Chest

By Charlaine Taylor

She lie dying. I was eight.
I sat on a hard backed chair,
My legs crossed at the ankles.
Quietly she dies in silence.
" She seldom speaks." I was told.
I sat there waiting, watching her.
Then she reached out her pale hand,
In that special way she had
Of crossing her fingers just so
To let me know she wanted me
To hold her hand. I stretched my hand
Down close to her bed covers.
Her hand reached way out to me.
She spoke after a long, long while.
Her voice came through walls of stillness
And slipped by like pillow cases
Pulled neatly over pillows.
Her head was on the pillow slips
That her hands had busily
Embroidered and crocheted
When she was a young girl.
Were they sewn only
For these dying moments?
She said: " This is exactly
What happens, just this."She spoke
Between long weighted pauses of
Deliberation like an epitaph.
" We don't use the contents of
Our hope chests, do we child?
This is the first time the things
In my hope chest have been used.
Remember, take the beauty
You have to give, use it,
Share it freely, my child. Keep
This secret locked in your
Hope chest and remember."

I thought then that age and
Dying gave wisdom." Grandmother,
Why don't any men have hope
Chests? " She replied with laughter,
" Probably because, child, they
Are credited with more brains. "
Grandmother had the answers.

The Long Journey

By Charlaine Taylor

It won't be deterred,
This little bird.
Bit by bit it keeps flying.
From the ground way low,
Toward the sky it keeps trying.
Once there see it go
Back and forth with a tune,
Because it can't be too soon.
This sparrow has its goal,
Fluffs its feathers to go.
It knows at last call
That the journey is all.

The Secret

By Charlaine Taylor

" The secret's in the
Martini and Rossie,
A whisper of vermouth:
Not more, but less is right,"
He says, as the hostess,
Carefully schooled, pours.
" The secret is in
The distant voices
Calling to everyone,
But him, as he stands,
Distant and alone,"
He says of the main
Character in 'Portrait
Of The Artist As A
Young Man.' "The secret
When being by yourself,
Separate and apart,
Is not to give up hope,"
He says, "Knowing that your
Greatest hope lies in
Believing in that hope,
And in yourself, your
Ability to gain,
To achieve what you dream
In your dream of dreams,
And with all your soul.
Then you are free to
Win it. It is yours: win.
The secret is in
Knowing this and yourself."
He says. We toast to that.
Here's to the secret of
The perfect martini,
And to your own life.
Here's to the secret of
'The Red Badge Of Courage'
Courage is the secret.

These Too Shall Pass Away

By Charlaine Taylor

They lasted two weeks more,
Twirls and circles galore.
She followed them with her eyes.
Ribbons alone stopped their rise.

They were meant to go higher,
Three balloons sailing by her.
Beyond her reach they'd go,
If they weren't held in tow.

They were made to be free,
Filled with what they couldn't be:
Held by the strings attached;
Tugging to be detached.

No doubt they could reach the sky
And continue up, so high,
Because they were not earth bound,
They would not touch the ground.

She wanted to aid their flight
And watch them go from her sight,
Colors flashing in the sun
Rising above everyone.

This is how it should be
For those meant to be free,
Beautiful in their flight
Until they were out of sight.

Nothing should bind them to earth,
Sailing for all they're worth.
Where would they land, if they land?
Off they go, out of hand.

Re: 3 mylar balloons, helium filled.

Trust Is That Hard Word

By Charlaine Taylor

Loyalty is that hard word
That goes with that hard word: trust.
They can be simulated,
But that attempt cannot last,
Before the truth appears
Shining its light on pure sham,
Which can abolish happiness
Long before you know it's gone.
Sometimes there's not enough time
To remember loyalty
And put it into practice.
Don't let it fall in the mud,
Then bow low to retrieve it.
It's too high for you to reach.
You don't want to take the pain
To win the bright victory.
Loyalty is that hard word.

Other Works By
Robert Goodwin Olmsted

Lines, A Book of Poetry
Published 2006

Breinigsville, PA USA
08 January 2010
230364BV00002B/22/P